This book belongs to

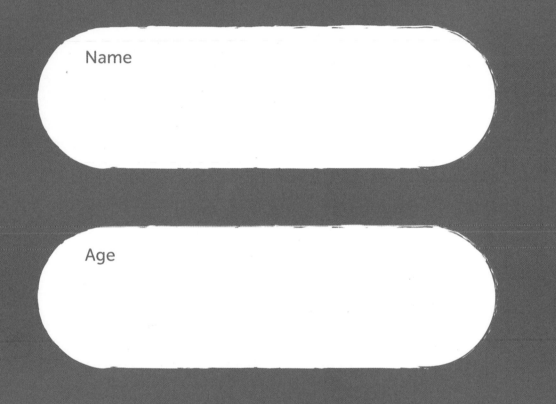

Name

Age

Save this book and all your amazing artwork
until you're all grown up!

はって Hatte © La Zoo 2010
First published in Japan in 2010 by Gakken Education Publishing Co., Ltd., Tokyo
Published in English by Downtown Bookworks Inc. by arrangement with Gakken Plus Co., Ltd.
English edition copyright Downtown Bookworks Inc. © 2017

Created and illustrated by La Zoo
Translated from the Japanese edition by Noriko Yoshimura

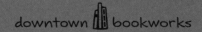

Downtown Bookworks Inc.
265 Canal Street
New York, NY 10013
www.downtownbookworks.com
Printed in China
October 2017
978-1941367490
10 9 8 7 6 5 4 3 2 1

If you can cut or tear paper, you can make beautiful art!

■ This book includes "starter art"—the beginnings of collages that you will complete with cut or torn paper. The only tools you need are scissors or your hands and glue.

● You can use any shapes you want—there are no mistakes when you make art. Be sure to keep any unused scraps for future creations.

♕ If you're able to write your name, be sure to sign your creations.

It's easy to use this book.

Before you start each picture, remove the collage paper from the book. You can cut or tear it out along the cut line.

In this example, you would use the paper to make feathers for the birds.

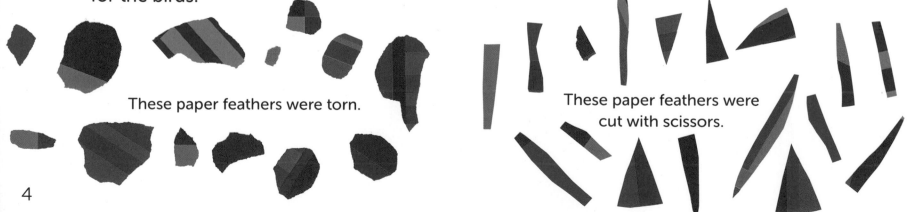

These paper feathers were torn.

These paper feathers were cut with scissors.

Paste the feathers onto each bird's body.

It's fine if the feathers stick out beyond the pages of the book. (It might look like the birds are flying!)

It's OK if you want to tear out more feathers from newspapers, magazines, catalogs, or any scrap paper you have at home.

Design your very own one-of-a-kind bird!

Every project comes with suggested directions, but you should have fun coming up with your own ideas as well. Make any shapes you want!

On this page, you can make hair, hats, horns—or anything else you like!

We need some more hair. Cut or tear the paper into different types of hair—curly, wavy, spiky, or any style you choose.

These guys could use some crowns. Cut the paper into crown shapes and glue them onto these kids' heads to make them look royally fancy.

20

23

When you make snail shells, you will find the outlines on the back of the collage paper.

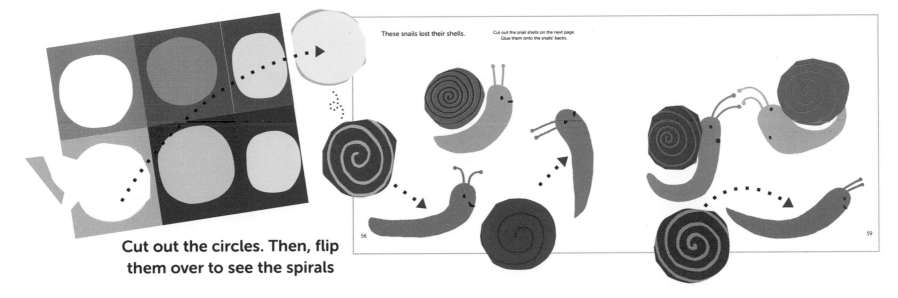

Cut out the circles. Then, flip them over to see the spirals

You'll also make ghosts! They can be happy or scary or anything else you decide. Add eyes and a mouth. Or don't. It's up to you!

It's all up to you! You decide what to create and how to create it.
YOU are the artist!

These birds need feathers to fly.

Cut or tear the colorful paper into feathers of different sizes and shapes. Then, paste them onto the birds.

You can even layer the feathers on top of each other. (Real birds have lots and lots of feathers.)

Cut the paper along this line and detach it from the book first.
It will make it easier to cut out or tear the page into feathers.

Give this bird a long tail feather.

Let the sun shine in!

Tear or cut the paper into rays of sunshine. Glue them around the sun.

Make this flower bloom.

Tear or cut the paper into petals and glue them into place to make a beautiful flower.

Give the squirrel a tail.

Tear or cut the paper into tails and glue them into place.

16

Give these squirrels nice tails, too.

Some squirrels have long tails. Some tails are round and bushy. And some tails curl up. Create whatever size and shape you like.

19

We need some more hair.

Cut or tear the paper into different types of hair—curly, wavy, spiky, or any style you choose.

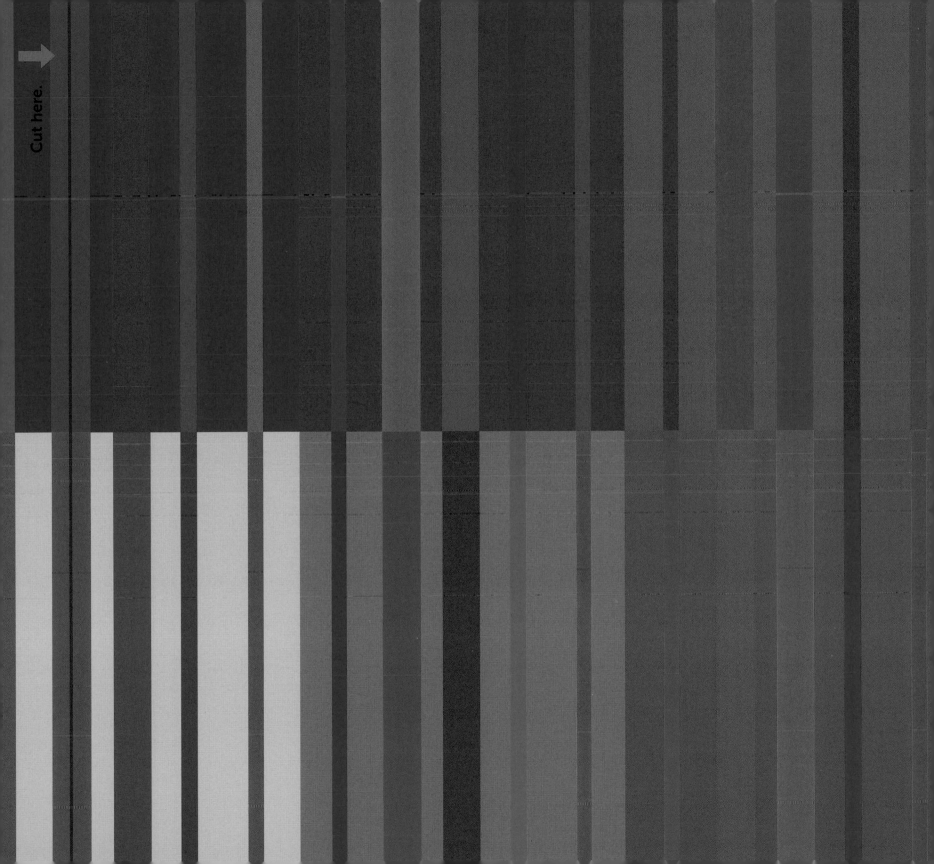

Cut here.

These guys could use some crowns. Cut the paper into crown shapes and glue them onto these kids' heads to make them look royally fancy.

These monkeys are embarrassed about something. Their cheeks are blushing.

Cut out some circles and paste them onto the monkey's cheeks.

24

Some monkeys have
red bottoms!

27

Hats off to you!

Cut out the hats from the next page and paste them onto these people's heads.

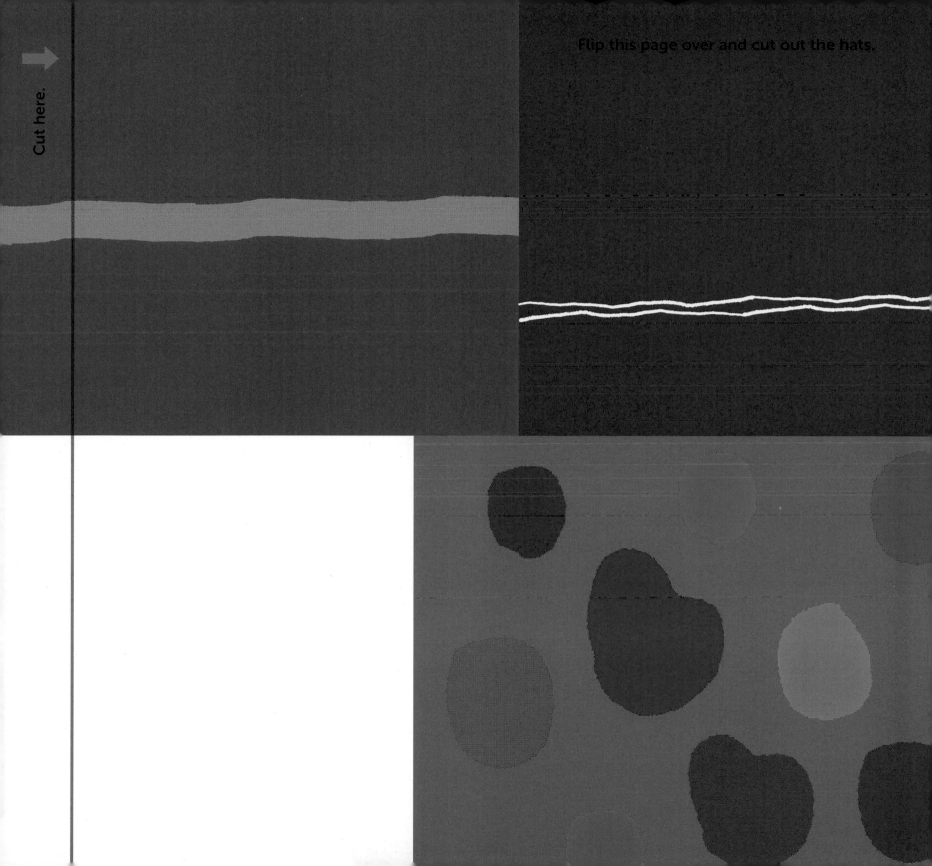

Cut here.

Flip this page over and cut out the hats.

Cut out the hats.

These fish need some scales.

Tear or cut the collage paper into different shapes. Then, paste them onto the fish. Layer as many scales as you like.

These pants are made for hopping.

Tear or cut the paper into little frog pants and paste them onto the frogs' legs.

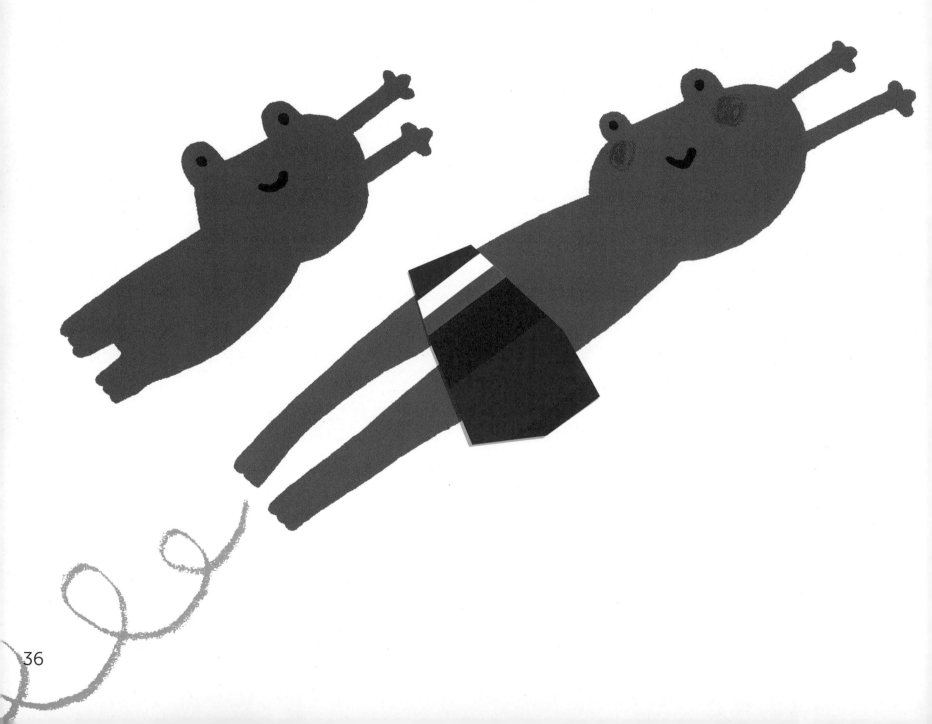

36

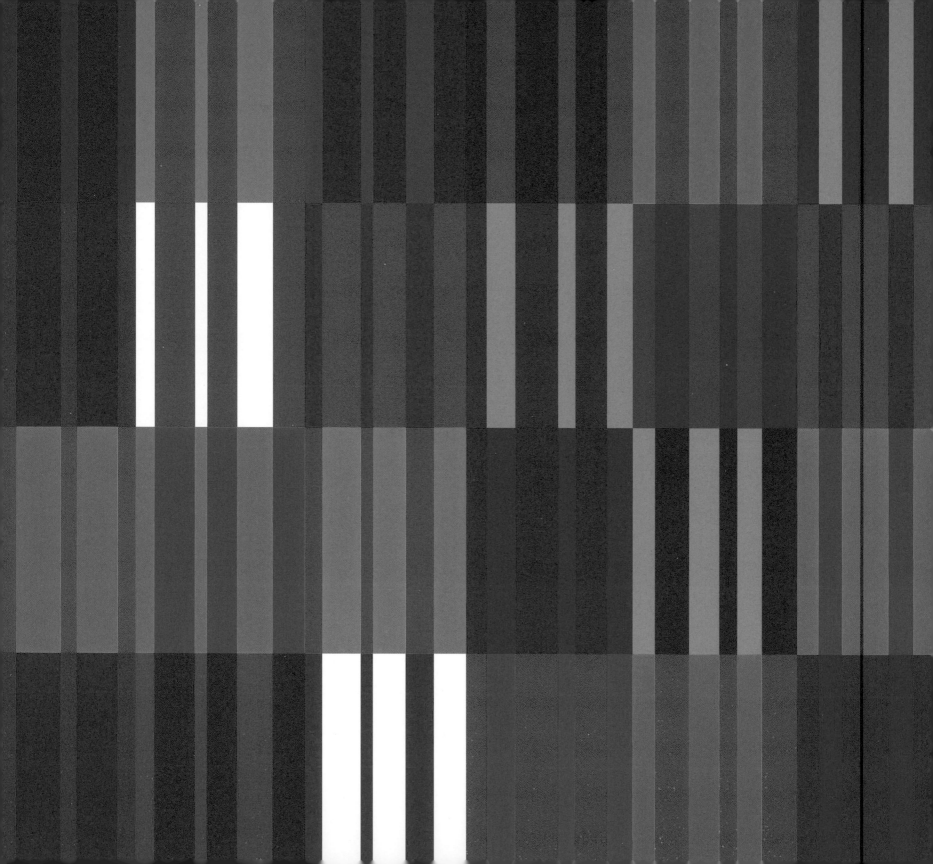

These frogs are going for a swim...

...and they need some swimsuits. Can you cut out swimsuits and paste them onto the frogs?
They may want hats, sunglasses, and beach bags too. You decide.

These branches are bare.

Tear or cut the paper into lots and lots of leaves and paste them onto the tree.

Cut here. →

Trees are much happier when they're covered with leaves.

Wrap the babies in their blankets.

Cut the paper into comfy bedding and paste it onto the babies to keep them warm.

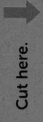

Cut here.

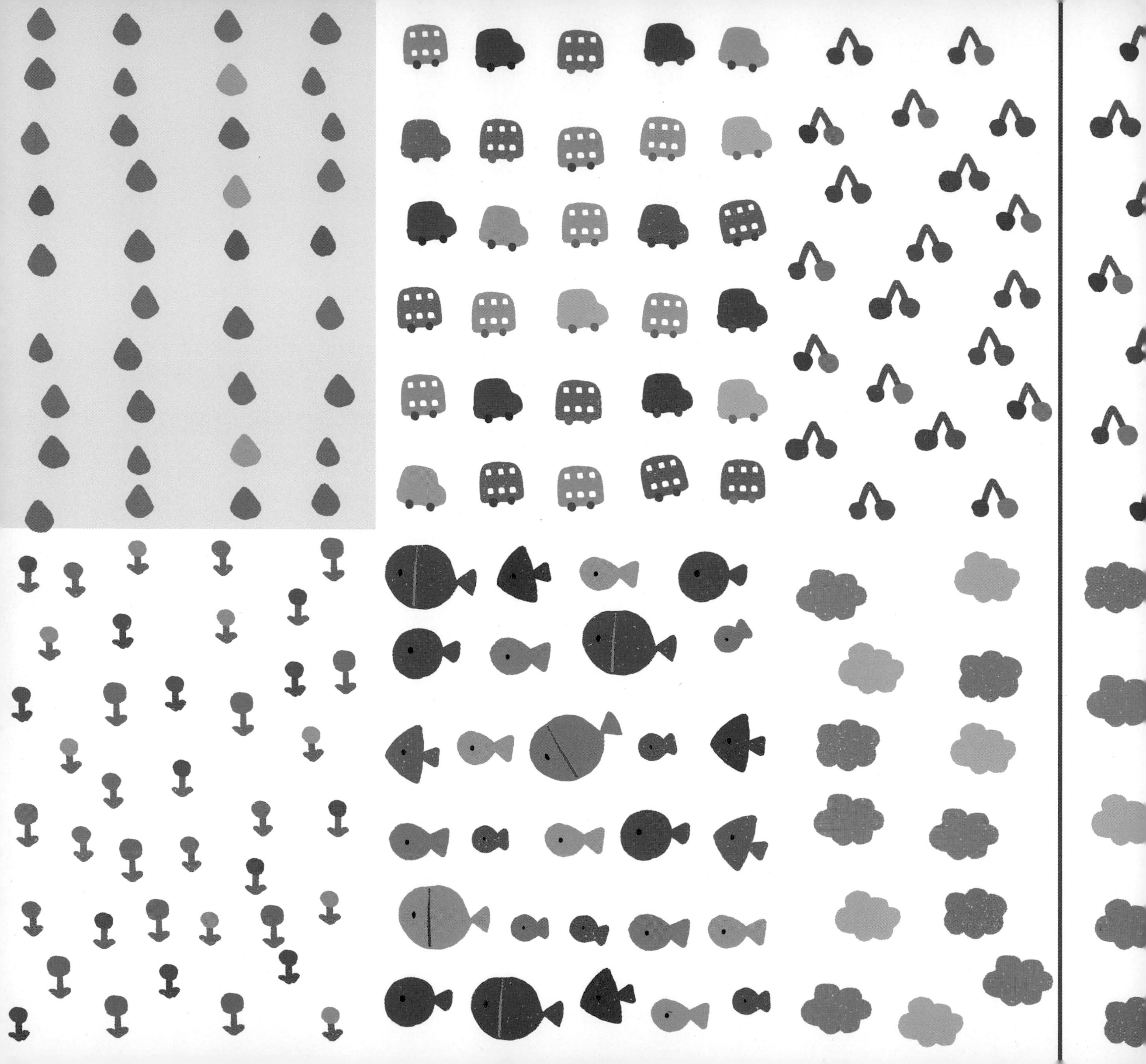

These babies need some cozy blankets too.

Strawberry shortcake! Can you decorate the cake with strawberries?

Cut the paper into strawberry shapes and place them all over the cake.

The more strawberries, the more delicious this cake will be!

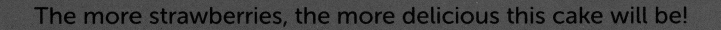

Reindeer always like to dress up when they go out.

Cut the paper into bows and ribbons and glue them onto the reindeer's antlers.

Cut here.

This reindeer wants to get dressed up too.

These snails lost their shells.

Cut out the snail shells on the next page.
Glue them onto the snails' backs.

Cut out these spirals by following the outlines on the other side of this page.

Cut out the circles below.

Stormy weather ahead!

Use scissors to cut the paper into zigzag shapes like lightning bolts. Then paste the lightning bolts onto the stormy sky.

Paste huge lightning bolts in the sky over the town.

Ouch! Someone has some boo-boos.

Cut the paper into strips and paste them over each of the wounds.

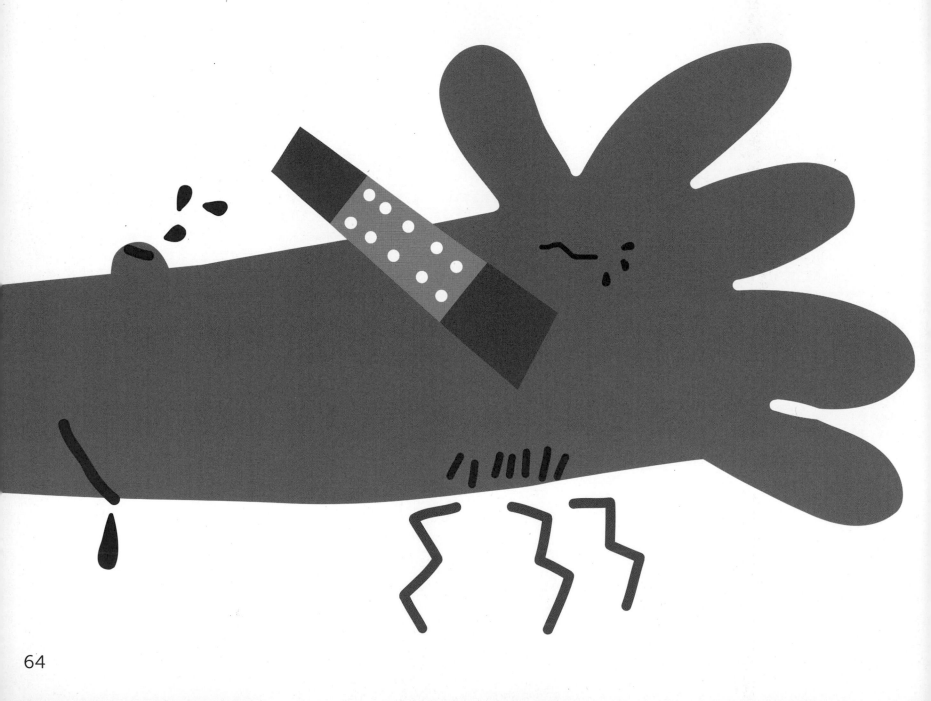

64

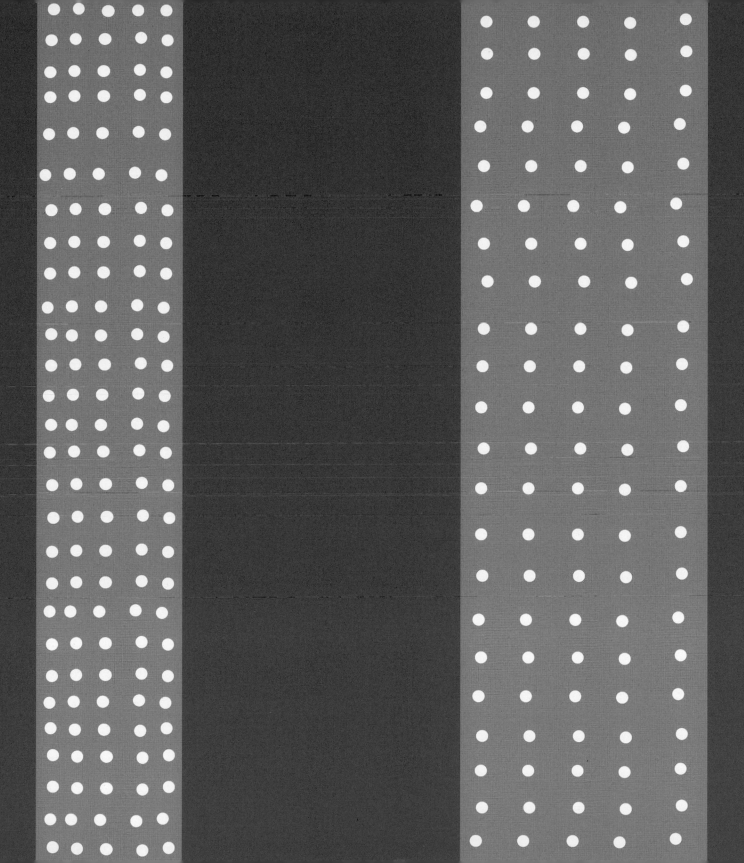

Cut here.

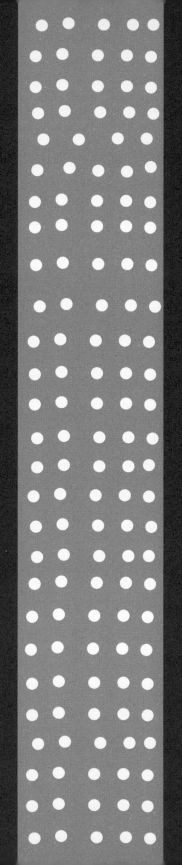

Yowza...this really hurts! Bandage up all of the cuts.

Fill the sky with fluffy clouds.

Cut clouds from the white paper and decorate the sky.

Fill the sky with fluffy clouds.

Give the acorns a bed of fallen leaves.

For more realistic-looking
leaves, rip up the paper,
crumple it, and then smooth
it before pasting.

72

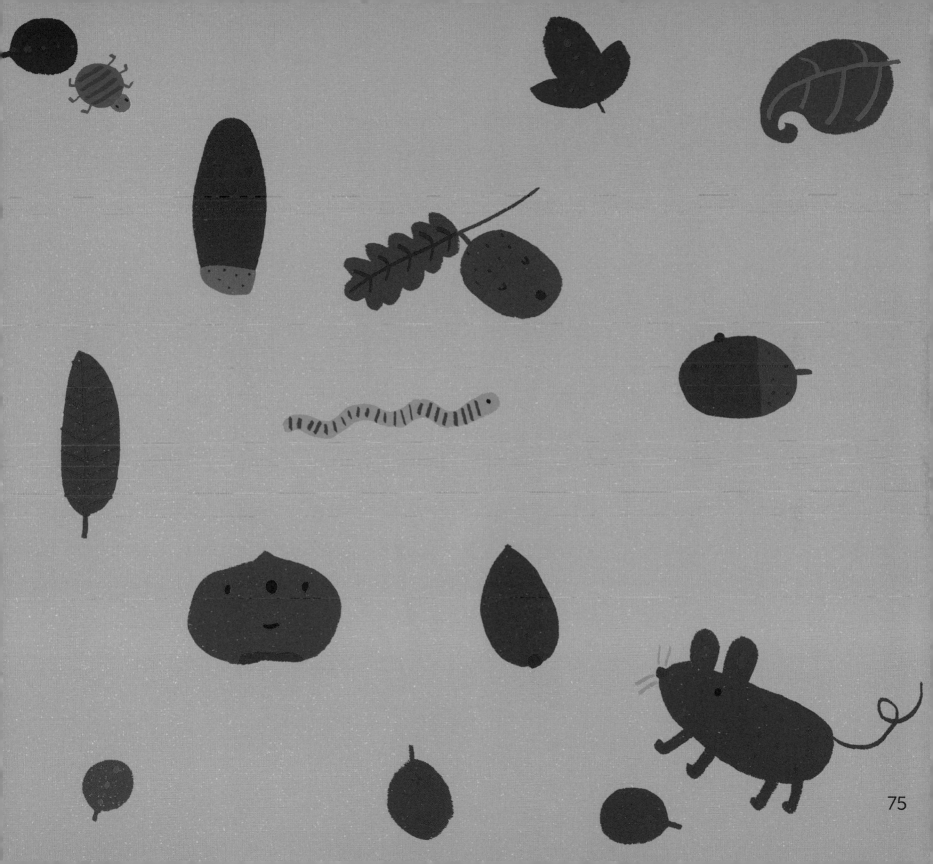

What's growing in the garden?

Rip the paper into small pieces to make petals. Glue them onto the stems to make a colorful bouquet.

Cut here.

Decorate the hedgehog's quills with flowers too!

It's party time!

Cut the paper into banners, streamers, and flags to make a festive scene on the page.

Have fun making banners and flags in lots of shapes and sizes.

You're a pizza chef. YUM!

Make a pizza by cutting out the peppers, tomatoes, and cheese and pasting them on top of the pizza crust! (Don't eat it!)

Cut here.

Cut the green paper into thin pepper strips.

Tear up the yellow paper, mixing up the sizes to make it look like gooey melted cheese.

Cut out the tomato shapes.

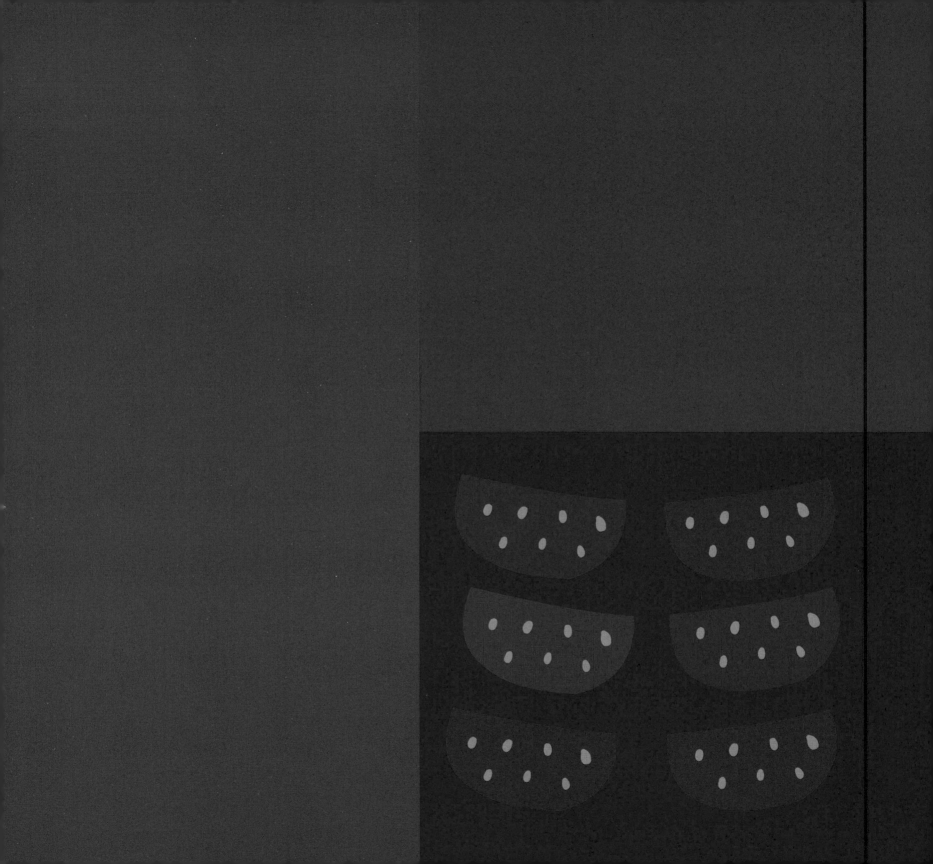

Put your pizza onto the plate. It's ready to eat!

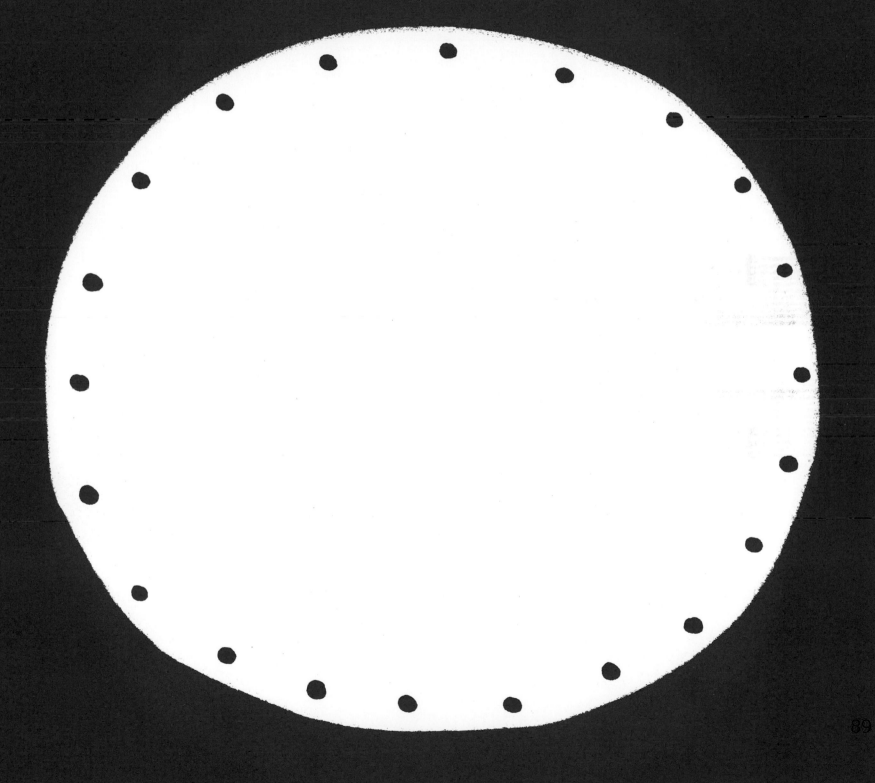

Sew buttons onto the pretty dress.

Cut here.

Cut out the shapes shown on the back of this page to make buttons.

Cut out the shapes below to make lots of little buttons.

Buttons make this dress look extra special.

What is going on inside the house?

Cut out the windows on the next page to create your very own dream house.

Cut out the shapes shown on the back of this page to make lots of fun windows.

Cut out the squares below to make
many different windows.

The bus needs windows too!

Give the elephant a very long trunk.

Tear the gray paper into a nice, long trunk and glue it onto the elephant's face.

What kind of trunk does this elephant have? Short or long?
Straight or curved? You decide!

BOO! Who is haunting this picture?

Rip the paper into different shapes and sizes. Draw eyes and mouths on the white shapes to make them look like ghosts!

Some ghosts are scary, but others are friendly. Fill the page with as many different ghosts as you can dream up.

I can build a town!

Cut out the buildings, cars, and trees. Then, glue them onto the page to design your own town.

Cut out the squares on the other side of this paper.

To make the buildings stand up, fold along the dotted lines and
then glue the smaller section of the paper onto the town.

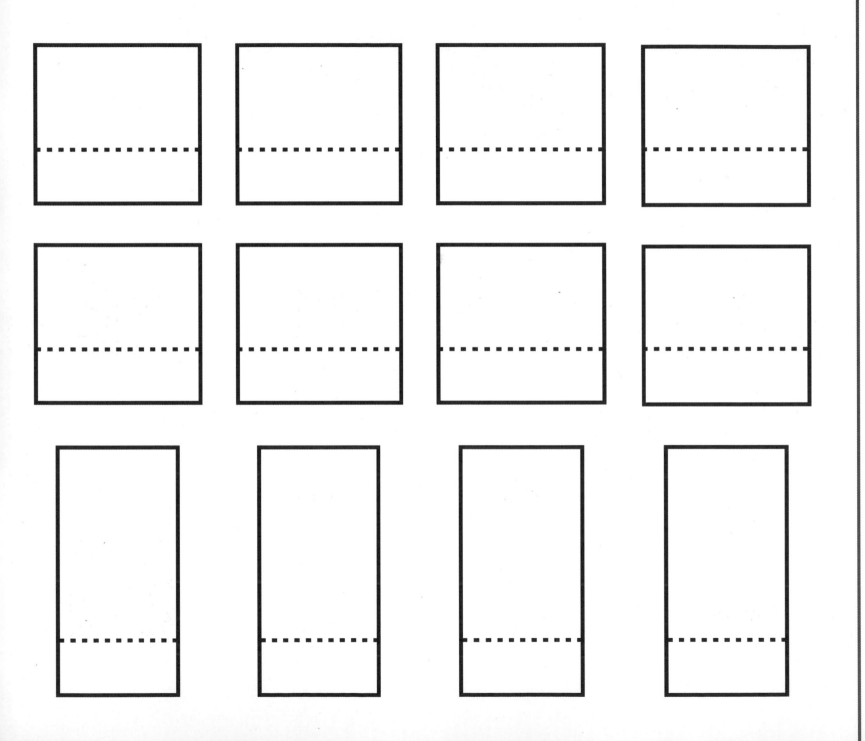

Cut out the squares below. To make the trees and cars stand up, fold
along the dotted lines and glue the smaller section onto the town.

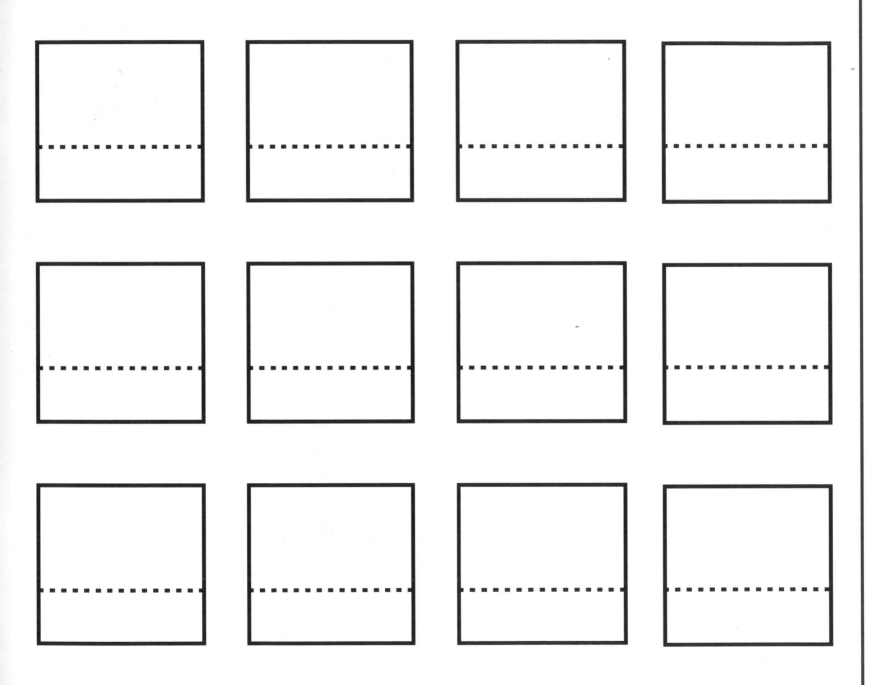

111

Can you find the ladybug?

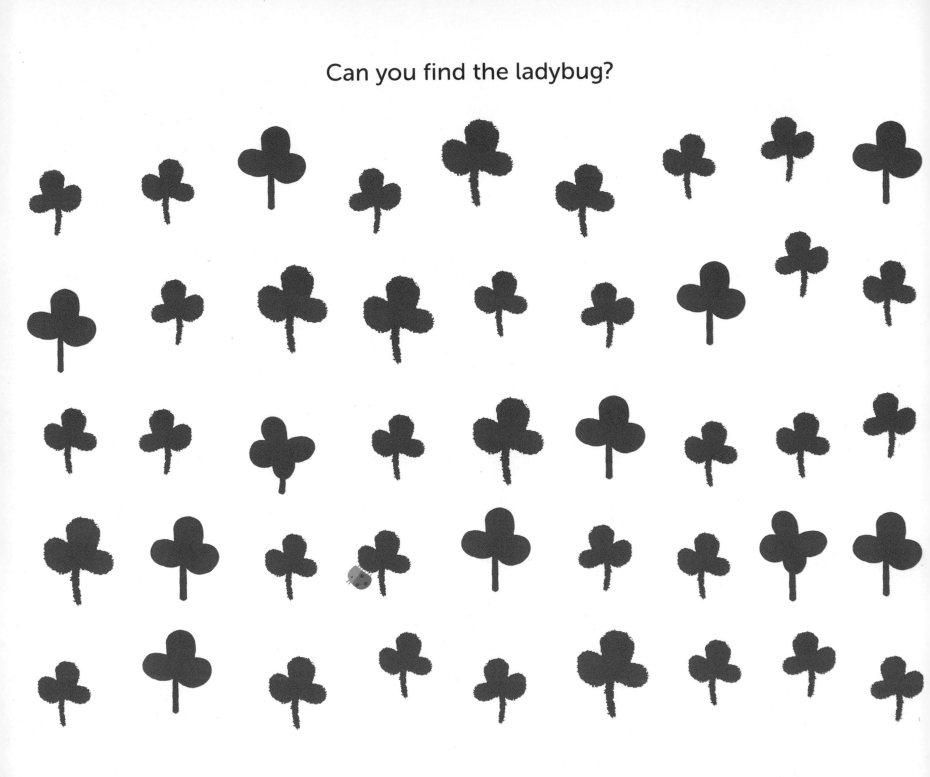